MODERN ROLE MODELS

Steve Nash

Ian Kimmich

Mason Crest Publishers

Produced by OTTN Publishing in association with
21st Century Publishing and Communications, Inc.

MASON CREST PUBLISHERS INC.
370 Reed Road
Broomall, Pennsylvania 19008
(866) MCP-BOOK (toll free)
www.masoncrest.com

Printed in the United States of America.

First Printing

9 8 7 6 5 4 3 2 1

Library of Congress Cataloging-in-Publication Data

Kimmich, Ian.
  Steve Nash / by Ian Kimmich.
    p. cm.
  Includes bibliographical references.
  ISBN-13: 978-1-4222-0485-6 (hardcover) — ISBN-13: 978-1-4222-0773-4 (pbk.)
  ISBN-10: 1-4222-0485-5 (hardcover)
  1. Nash, Steve, 1974–   —Juvenile literature. 2. Basketball players—Canada—
Biography—Juvenile literature. I. Title.
  GV884.N37K56 2009
  796.323092—dc22
  [B]   2008020413

Publisher's note:
All quotations in this book come from original sources, and contain the spelling
and grammatical inconsistencies of the original text.

CROSS-CURRENTS

*In the ebb and flow of the currents of life we are each influenced
by many people, places, and events that we directly experience
or have learned about. Throughout the chapters of this book you
will come across **CROSS-CURRENTS** reference boxes. These
boxes direct you to a **CROSS-CURRENTS** section in the back
of the book that contains fascinating and informative sidebars
and related pictures. Go on. ▸▸*

CONTENTS

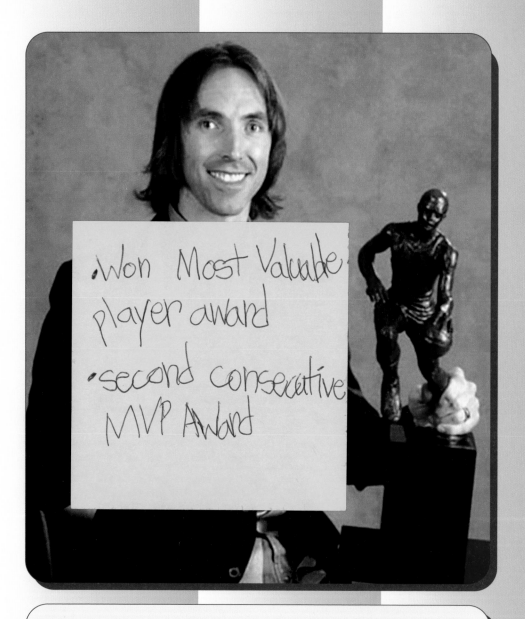

Steve Nash poses with the Maurice Podoloff Trophy, 2006. The trophy is given each year to the NBA's Most Valuable Player, and Steve is flashing two fingers in the photo to indicate that this is his second consecutive MVP award. That feat put him in elite company: in the history of the NBA, only 10 other players had won multiple MVPs.

1

Kid Canadian Becomes Mr. MVP

ON MAY 24, 2006, AFTER ADVANCING THROUGH two hard-fought rounds of the National Basketball Association playoffs, the Phoenix Suns faced the powerhouse Dallas Mavericks in the first game of the Western Conference Finals. Before the game, the NBA awarded its trophy for the Most Valuable Player of the 2005–2006 regular season. The recipient was Suns captain Steve Nash.

After the pregame ceremony was over and the Suns and Mavericks took the floor, Nash—one of only a handful of Canadians ever to play in the NBA—put on a true MVP performance. He did what all NBA coaches hope their **point guard** can do: control the flow of the game. Sometimes Steve pushed the ball down the court, helping his team score easy baskets in the **transition offense**. Other times he slowed down the pace and directed Phoenix's **set offense**. With his extraordinary ball-handling skills and quickness, he frequently beat his man. If he got an open look at the basket, Steve pulled up for a jump shot or lofted a running one-hander as he sliced through the lane. If a Dallas defender [He averaged 20 points] the ball off to the open [and 10 assists] powered the Suns to a 12 [per game.]

⇒ "ONE [ ]R" ⇐

Despite its Gam[ ]ding play throughout the [ ]Mavericks. Dallas won the [ ]dvance to the NBA Finals.

Still, fans, o[ ]ut admire Steve's gritty pe[ ]e averaged more than 20 p[ ]he raised the level of play [ ]mmented:

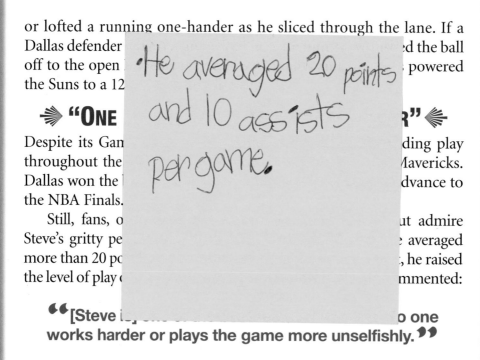

> **66** [Steve is, ... o one works harder or plays the game more unselfishly. **99**

That work ethic and unselfish play—hallmarks of Steve Nash's brand of basketball—were major reasons why Phoenix had an outstanding 2005–2006 season, and why Nash was named league MVP. Of course, the Suns' point guard also posted some outstanding individual statistics that year. He led all NBA players in assists, averaging 10.5 per game. He also averaged 18.8 points and 4.2 rebounds per game, both career highs. Steve burnished his credentials as one of the game's most accurate shooters, hitting on 51.2 percent of his **field goal** attempts— including 43.9 percent from three-point range—and sinking a league-best 92.1 percent of his **free throws**.

The NBA is pro basketball's most elite league. Each year, 360 of the best players in the world find a roster spot on one of the league's 30 teams. Being selected the NBA's MVP is a rare honor—recognition that, considering all facets of the game, the player has performed better than all of his peers over the course of an entire season. But by winning MVP honors in 2005–2006, Steve Nash joined an even more elite group: players who were judged best of the best for more than one year running. In garnering his first league MVP trophy, for the 2004–2005 season, Steve posted a league-leading 11.5 assists per game, shot 50.2 percent from the field, and led his team to a 62-20 record, the best the NBA had seen in 10 years. The Suns also reached the Western Conference Finals.

As Dirk Nowitzki looks on, Steve Nash drives around Keith Van Horn of the Dallas Mavericks during Game 3 of the Western Conference Finals, May 28, 2006. Steve led his Phoenix Suns with 21 points and seven assists, but the Mavericks won the game, 95-88, to take a two-games-to-one series lead.

Charlotte Bobcats forward Gerald Wallace attempts to stop Steve Nash from driving to the basket during a 2006 game. Defending Steve is a difficult task: he has excellent quickness, can drive to his right or left equally well, is an accurate shooter, and is one of the best passers in the NBA.

The fact that the Suns went deep into the playoffs during Steve's back-to-back MVP seasons was no accident, and it validated his selection as MVP. Basketball is a team sport, and the greatest players in the game contribute more than big individual statistics. They make their teammates better and help their teams win. Steve Nash's value goes beyond his individual stats, impressive though they are.

CROSS-CURRENTS

To learn about other players who have won the NBA's Most Valuable Player award more than once, read "MVPs in Multiples." Go to page 48.

⇒ THE MARK OF NASH ⇐

Unlike some other superstars, Steve has never disrespected other players or the game. And despite his great success, he remains humble. Typical is a statement he made to the Canadian Broadcasting Corporation:

> **"A lot is made about me making my teammates better, and I really believe that my teammates make me a lot better, too."**

Steve's weapons on the basketball court are numerous. He has outstanding quickness, and he dribbles equally well with both hands, allowing him to penetrate defenses and to direct Phoenix's fast-paced "run-and-gun" offense. His vision on the court is extraordinary, enabling him to spot open teammates. And Steve is one of the best passers in the game.

But beyond these physical skills and abilities, it is Steve's mental toughness that has helped him become one of the NBA's premier players. His confidence is unshakeable. Even if he has had a subpar night shooting the ball, when the game is on the line, he still looks to take the big shot—and more often than not, he delivers. When asked by interviewer Charlie Rose about his approach to the game, Steve explained:

> **"I just try to, you know, be mentally strong and nothing is going to set me back, nothing is going to bother me. I'm going to be—stay the course."**

Steve Nash knows only one way to play basketball: by bringing all his skill, energy, and dedication to every game. This attitude has made him a favorite of fans, coaches, teammates, and even opponents.

Steve Nash developed a love for soccer during his childhood in Canada, and he remains an avid recreational player today. In this photo, taken in August 2007 in New York City's Central Park, Steve (back row, fourth from left) poses with members of his amateur soccer club and players from the Red Bulls professional soccer team. The occasion was a friendly game.

2

The Rising Star

___

STEPHEN JOHN NASH WAS BORN IN JOHANNES- burg, South Africa, on February 7, 1974. His parents, John and Jean Nash, were both avid athletes—John played professional soccer (or football, as it is called outside the United States) in an English league, and Jean played on the English national **netball** team. They inspired their children to be healthy, to compete, and to enjoy the games they played.

When Steve was barely more than a year old, his parents moved their family out of South Africa, in part to escape **apartheid**. A policy of racial separation that was upheld through a series of unjust laws, apartheid was designed to keep power in the hands of South Africa's white minority. The country's nonwhite majority, meanwhile, suffered political and economic discrimination. By the 1970s, opposition to the system was leading to increasing violence in South Africa.

The Nashes moved halfway around the world and settled in the Canadian city of Victoria. It is the capital of the province of British Columbia.

➤ GROWING UP IN VICTORIA ➤

In Canada, Steve grew up breathing soccer. Because the field (called the "pitch") is so large, there is a lot of focus on accurate short and long passes. Steve later told the *Times of London*:

> **"Playing [soccer], I was always trying to find ways to chip balls, bend them, slip balls into gaps, so when I started playing basketball and was allowed to use my hands to do the same sort of things, it felt like cheating."**

Steve and his younger brother and sister each showed great skill on the pitch, and both of Steve's siblings still play. In addition to soccer, Steve excelled in hockey, baseball, lacrosse, and basketball, but he knew he couldn't play every sport all of the time.

In high school—he attended St. Michael's University School in Victoria—basketball became Steve's number-one sport, though he continued to play soccer as well. He quickly became the best basketball player St. Michael's had seen in a long time, and with hard work and determination he continued to improve. He later told the Canadian edition of *Time* magazine:

> **"A coach told me my left hand was a little shaky. That was the last time I was going to hear that."**

In his senior season, Steve averaged almost a **triple-double** in every game, with 21.3 points, 11.2 assists, and 9.1 rebounds. He led his team to win the British Columbia AAA Provincial Championship. To cap off the year, Steve was named British Columbia Player of the Year in both soccer and basketball.

During his senior season, Steve sent videos of his basketball highlights to numerous colleges and universities. At the time, though, few schools seriously considered non-U.S. players. The skinny 6'3" point guard from Canada was rejected or simply ignored by more than 30 American schools with basketball programs.

One coach, however, took notice of the tapes showing the kid from Victoria passing, shooting, and dribbling circles around bigger players. Santa Clara University's Dick Davey flew to Canada to pay a visit to Steve Nash. Impressed, he offered Steve a scholarship. Steve accepted, enrolling at Santa Clara, which is near San Jose, in the fall of 1992.

❧ CALIFORNIA DREAMS ❧

As if to prove his worth to all the schools that had rejected him, Steve began training harder than ever. He lived and breathed basketball, as Dick Davey observed:

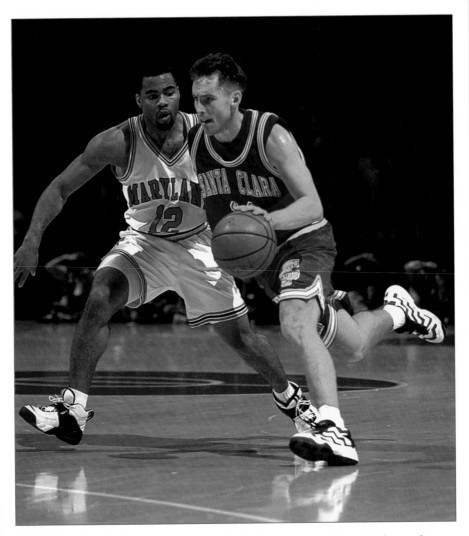

March madness: Steve Nash drives past the University of Maryland's Terrell Stokes in first-round action from the 1996 NCAA men's basketball tournament. Steve's Santa Clara Broncos upset the Terps in the game but were bounced from the tournament in the second round by the University of Kansas.

❝We'd practice all day, then he'd eat dinner and come back with five teammates to play 3-on-3. He made the other players deranged, too.❞

In his third year, Steve led the Santa Clara Broncos to a first-place finish in their conference and was named West Coast Conference Player of the Year. Santa Clara reached the 1995 NCAA men's basketball tournament as a #12 **seed**. But the **underdog** Broncos lost in the first round to 5th-seeded Mississippi State.

CROSS-CURRENTS

For more details about Steve's experiences in the NCAA men's basketball tournament, read "March Madness." Go to page 50. ▶▶

Steve Nash was used to being an underdog—and he loved proving critics wrong. In his senior year of college, Steve put together his best season, setting school records in total assists, three-pointers made, and free throw percentage. His team again won the West Coast Conference, and he was again named Conference Player of the Year. In the 1996 NCAA tournament, the 10th-seeded Broncos engineered a first-round upset of 7th-seeded Maryland. But Steve and Santa Clara were stopped in the second round by a powerhouse Kansas team.

⧽ SHOOTING FOR THE NBA ⧼

Though his team failed to play deep into college basketball's ultimate tournament, Steve Nash's skills on the court drew the attention of pro scouts. In the 1996 NBA draft, he was chosen 15th overall by the Phoenix Suns.

CROSS-CURRENTS

The 1996 NBA draft is considered one of the best in history. To learn more, check out "In with the New." Go to page 51. ▶▶

Phoenix, however, already had two All-Star point guards—Kevin Johnson and Jason Kidd—and Steve sat on the bench for most of his rookie season, producing only a few points and assists in his meager playing time. Suns fans didn't think much of the team's new recruit, but Steve never let their boos affect his confidence. In fact, he reacted to the criticism just as he always had—by working even harder to improve. Teammate Kevin Johnson said of Steve Nash:

❝He used to drill us in practice. By the midway point of his first year, he was the best point guard on the team.❞

Wearing a cap with the logo of his new team, Steve Nash poses for a publicity photo shortly after being selected in the first round of the NBA's 1996 draft. The Phoenix Suns drafted Steve with the 15th overall pick. Two other future MVPs were drafted ahead of Steve: Allen Iverson (the first overall pick) and Kobe Bryant (the 13th).

Still, the Suns failed to find a place for Steve in the starting lineup. In the summer of 1998, after his sophomore season, Steve was traded to the Dallas Mavericks. If he had yet to find stardom in the NBA, at least he would be making a lot of money: Steve's six-year contract with Dallas was worth $33 million.

Traded to the Dallas Mavericks after the 1998–1999 season, Steve initially got a chilly reception from the hometown fans. Many didn't think the Canadian's brief career in the NBA justified his six-year, $33 million salary. But the Mavericks' faithful soon came to appreciate Steve's unselfish style of play and his ability to direct the offense from the point-guard position.

3

From Dallas to the World

FANS IN DALLAS GAVE STEVE NASH A COLD welcome when he arrived in town. Many didn't believe that Steve's unproven talent justified his big contract. And as had been the case in Phoenix, Steve would have to compete for playing time with two other established point guards, Erick Strickland and Robert Pack.

Again Steve had to fight an uphill battle against his critics. But he didn't mind. In recalling the way he was greeted by the rabid Dallas fans, Steve told the Canadian edition of *Time*:

> **"**I didn't take it as the end of the world. I took it as, 'How many people get a chance to be booed by 20,000 people?' As stupid or perverse as that sounds, I took it as a great opportunity to overcome something.**"**

⇒ YEAR OF THE LOCKOUT ⇐

Before the start of the 1998–1999 season—Steve's first in a Dallas Mavericks uniform—the NBA and the players' union failed to come to an agreement on the general terms of player contracts. To put pressure on the union, team owners used a tactic known as a lockout. Unlike a strike, in which employees refuse to work at their jobs, a lockout occurs when business owners refuse to let their employees work. The NBA canceled games and even prohibited players from using **franchise** facilities to practice. After months of wrangling, an agreement was finally reached, but the season didn't begin until February 5, 1999. The usual 82-game schedule had to be shortened to only 50 games in the regular season.

The time off didn't do Steve Nash or the Dallas Mavericks any good. Steve received more playing time but recorded fewer points and assists per game than he had in Phoenix. Dallas fans booed Steve almost every time he stepped on the court, but they may have been blaming him for the team's poor performance. The Mavericks finished the 1999 season with the terrible record of 19 wins and 31 losses.

Near the end of the already-shortened season, Steve suffered a lower back sprain, which forced him to sit out the last 10 games. He had a spinal condition known as spondylolisthesis, in which a **vertebra** slips forward over the vertebra beneath it. This causes tightened nerves in the back and hamstring, loss of movement, and great pain. Even now, a decade after the injury, Steve has to take very special care to stay loose. He is constantly moving during games, and when resting he often has to lie flat on the floor to keep his vertebrae in place.

⇒ TURNING DALLAS AROUND ⇐

Steve began the 1999–2000 season ready to do everything he could to help Dallas win. And win the Mavericks did. His skills at point guard helped unleash the offensive firepower of German-born big man Dirk Nowitzki and veteran shooting guard/forward Michael Finley. Once Dallas fans realized that Steve Nash was a team player, the boos stopped. Then, halfway through the season, Steve again had to sit out because of an injury. He ended up missing 25 games—about two months—as he recovered from a severe ankle sprain.

Dallas struggled while he was gone, and the team and fans were supportive when Steve returned to the lineup. He rewarded them by finishing the season strongly and scoring six **double-doubles** in

Steve guards Cuttino Mobely of the Houston Rockets in a game on December 30, 2000. By the 2000–2001 season, the Mavericks had made Steve their starting point guard. He responded with fine offensive output, averaging 15.6 points and 7.3 assists per game over the course of the season.

the final weeks of the season. Nevertheless, the Mavericks finished with a 40-42 record and just missed the playoffs.

⇒ THE SUMMER OLYMPIAN ⇐

Coming off the best season of his young career, Steve's next challenge waited in Sydney, Australia, where he played for Team Canada in the 2000 Summer Olympics. Steve Nash was already a household name in his home country, and the Canadian team gave its star a first-class ticket to

CROSS-CURRENTS

If you would like to learn more about some popular basketball statistics, check out "Statistics of Dominance." Go to page 52. ▶▶

Sydney and a hotel suite all to himself. While he kept the airline ticket, Steve insisted on sharing a regular room with a teammate, just like all the other players. In addition to setting this example, Steve bestowed on his teammates a generous gift. To everyone who wasn't in the NBA, he gave $3,000 for spending money in Australia.

CROSS-CURRENTS

For some history and additional information about basketball on the international stage, read "World Hoops." Go to page 53. ▶▶

Steve's efforts at building team morale paid dividends. Behind his strong performances, Team Canada finished with five wins and two losses—Canada's best Olympic men's basketball record in more than half a century. Canada was eliminated in the quarterfinals by the French team that went on to win the silver medal.

⋙ LIFE OF THE STAR ⋘

The 2000–2001 season saw a new Steve Nash. He played with even more skill and awareness, and he sported a new, wavy hairstyle. His hair seemed to take on a personality of its own. When asked by the *Sporting News* about people's comments on his hair, Steve said:

> **❝I really don't care what people's response is, this is just how my hair is. I don't take care of it, or comb it, or put anything in it, or style it or anything . . . it is funny to me that it draws such attention. It makes me realize how insignificant that sort of thing is, how silly it is to get carried away by that.❞**

Steve also seemed to take to the nightlife in Dallas a bit more than he had in Phoenix. Occasionally, celebrity magazines published rumors linking him romantically with famous women, including actress Elizabeth Hurley and singers Nelly Furtado and Geri Halliwell (Ginger Spice of the Spice Girls). Steve denied those rumors. In 2001, he met Alejandra Amarilla, who became his longtime girlfriend and, later, his wife.

⋙ ON POINT IN DALLAS ⋘

With his big, new hair, Steve was ready for his big, new role. Over the next four seasons, he started every game in which he played—and for two of those seasons he played in all 82 games.

Showing tremendous body control and fearlessness in going to the basket, Steve Nash splits two Philadelphia 76ers defenders in a game at Philadelphia's First Union Center, November 1, 2001. For the first time in his NBA career, Steve would play in all 82 regular-season games during the 2001–2002 season.

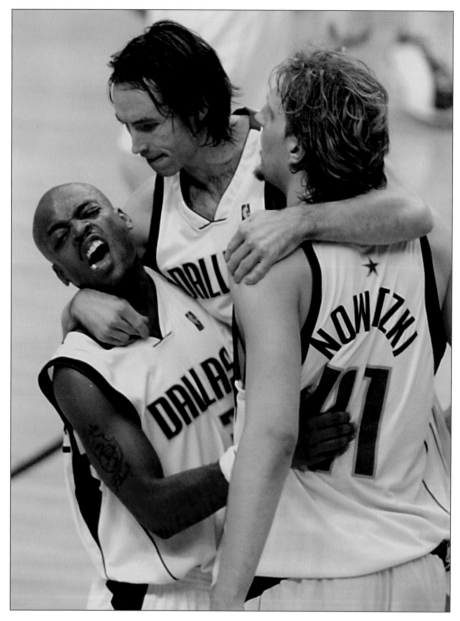

During a timeout in a 2003 game, Dallas teammates Nick Van Exel (left) and Dirk Nowitzki congratulate Steve Nash for making a great play. The Mavericks had much to celebrate during the 2002–2003 season: the team won 60 games, tying the San Antonio Spurs for the best record in the NBA.

The benefit Steve Nash brought to his team went beyond the numbers he produced. As he matured, Steve's playmaking abilities became so formidable that other teams always had to pay special attention to defending him. Thus, even on plays in which Steve didn't score or make an assist himself, he often created time and space for his teammates. He and Nowitzki strengthened their friendship and teamwork, practicing hard and watching soccer matches when relaxing.

During the 2000–2001 season, Steve's hard work paid off. He almost doubled his average points and assists per game from the previous year. And he led the Mavericks to the second round of the playoffs for the first time since 1988. After losing three straight games to the San Antonio Spurs, Dallas came out firing in Game 4. Steve racked up six assists on his team's first eight baskets, and the Mavericks pulled out a victory, 112-108. Unfortunately for Dallas fans, the team lost Game 5 and was eliminated.

Behind the solid play of Steve Nash and Dirk Nowitzki, the Mavericks put together a franchise-best season in 2001–2002, winning 57 games against only 25 losses. The Mavericks again made it to the Western Conference Semifinals, but again they sputtered, this time in the face of the superior defense of the Sacramento Kings.

As if to make up for their second early exit from the playoffs, the Mavericks began the 2002–2003 season with a 14-game winning streak and didn't look back, posting 60 wins and tying the Spurs for the best record in the NBA that year. Steve earned his second consecutive All-Star selection in 2003, making him the only Canadian two-time All-Star.

The test for dominance between the Mavericks and the Spurs came in the Western Conference Finals. After losing Nowitzki to a knee sprain in Game 3, Dallas entered Game 5 down three games to one. Paced by some clutch fourth-quarter shooting by Steve Nash, the Mavericks went on to win the contest. But the Spurs overwhelmed them, 90-78, in Game 6 and went on to win the NBA championship.

⟫ SHOOT FOR PEACE ⟪

In February 2003, as the NBA's top players converged on Atlanta for the All-Star Game, the United States seemed headed for a war in Iraq. The administration of President George W. Bush claimed that Iraq and its leader, Saddam Hussein, had been connected to the terrorist attacks of September 11, 2001. Many people—wrongly, as it turned out—believed this claim, as well as other reasons the Bush administration

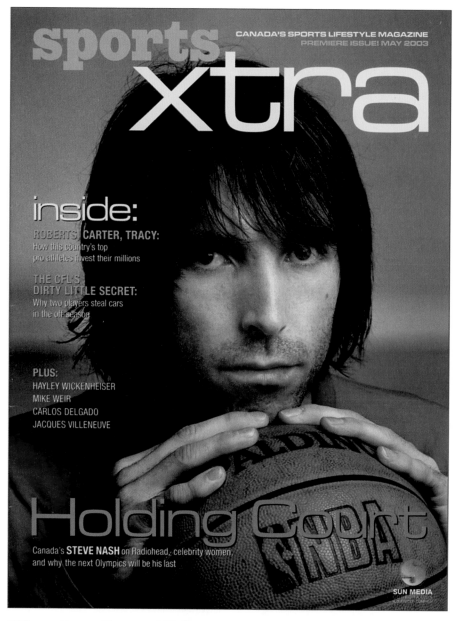

sports
xtra
CANADA'S SPORTS LIFESTYLE MAGAZINE
PREMIERE ISSUE! MAY 2003

inside:
ROBERTS, CARTER, TRACY:
How this country's top
pro athletes invest their millions

**THE CFL'S
DIRTY LITTLE SECRET:**
Why two players steal cars
in the off season

PLUS:
HAYLEY WICKENHEISER
MIKE WEIR
CARLOS DELGADO
JACQUES VILLENEUVE

Holding Court
Canada's **STEVE NASH** on Radiohead, celebrity women,
and why the next Olympics will be his last

SUN MEDIA

When Canadian publisher Sun Media launched a new sports/lifestyle magazine in May 2003, the editors put Steve Nash on the cover. In a profile inside the issue, the point guard candidly shared his views on topics ranging from his tastes in music to his opposition to the U.S.-led invasion of Iraq.

offered for invading Iraq. Other people, however, thought that a war with Iraq couldn't be justified. Steve Nash was one such person, and he decided not to remain silent. As the All-Star teams were warming up, Steve revealed the T-shirt he was wearing. Written across it were the words "No War—Shoot for Peace."

While some players and fans agreed with his anti–Iraq War sentiment, other people took issue. Former Spurs star David Robinson, a graduate of the United States Naval Academy who had served in the navy, slammed Steve. One journalist commented that Steve should just "shut up and play." Steve, however, doesn't believe in "shutting up" when he sees something he believes is wrong—he believes in speaking out. He told *Sports Illustrated*:

> **"I think a lot of what we hear in the news is misleading and flat-out false, so I think it's important for us to think deeper and find out what is really going on."**

⟫ CHANGING TERRAIN ⟪

The 2003–2004 season was one of transitions for Dallas, and Steve tried to find his place on the changing team. The Mavericks brought in more offensive firepower, and though Steve increased his assists, he scored fewer points. That probably was the reason he wasn't selected as an All-Star in 2004.

That year, Dallas exited the playoffs early, losing to the Sacramento Kings in the first round. Steve Nash was now a free agent, meaning he could sign a contract with any team that wanted him. The Phoenix Suns made Steve an offer of $65 million for five years.

Steve gave the Mavericks the opportunity to match the Suns' offer, but Dallas owner Mark Cuban didn't think his point guard was worth the money. After signing with Phoenix, Steve summed up his feelings:

> **"[Phoenix] wanted me. In Dallas, it was apparent I wasn't as important. It was disappointing, because we started something but we really didn't get a chance to finish it."**

Late in the summer of 2004, Steve packed his gear and headed back to the city where he had begun his NBA career.

Happy to be back in the Valley of the Sun: In 2004, at the age of 30, Steve Nash returned to Phoenix, where he'd begun his NBA career. Steve had been a free agent at the end of the 2003–2004 season, and Dallas Mavericks owner Mark Cuban made little effort to re-sign him. The Suns offered Steve a five-year contract worth $65 million.

The Valley of the Sun

IN PHOENIX, STEVE NASH CONTINUED HIS LIFE- long habit of working harder—and dramatically improving his game—whenever he felt someone had rejected him. In his first year back with the Suns, Steve showed Mavericks owner Mark Cuban what he could do. He played the best ball of his career, helping the Suns pile up wins during the regular season.

⇒ A NEW ROLE ⇐

When he joined the Suns in 2004, Steve was 30 years old. While that is young by the standards of everyday life, many pro basketball players see their productivity begin to tail off at or around age 30. Of course, Steve Nash is far from typical.

The Suns were a young team in 2004. The roster was filled with rookies and second-year players—and with the elder statesman Steve Nash. Midway through the 2004–2005 season, he told the *Sporting News*:

"When you think about it, it is really weird. I was just part of a bunch of guys in Dallas who came in together and helped change things. Now, it's a different role for me, all of a sudden. I can handle it, I understand it, but it is definitely different. I'm the old man here."

But Steve was used to being an experienced leader on and off the court, and right away he started helping design team and individual training programs.

CROSS-CURRENTS
To learn about the careers of some other great NBA point guards, check out "Running Point." Go to page 54. ▶▶

In addition to his new role on his new basketball team, Steve saw major changes in his personal life shortly after his arrival in Phoenix. On October 14, 2004, his longtime girlfriend, Alejandra Amarilla, gave birth to twin daughters. The couple named the girls Lourdes and Isabella, and Dirk Nowitzki became their godfather. Steve and Alejandra decided to wait until after the 2004–2005 season to get married (they were wed in June 2005).

⇒ IMMEDIATE IMPACT ⇐

Phoenix fans were happy to have Steve back—their days of booing him were long over. He was more mature, smarter on the court, and, if possible, more skilled than when the Suns traded him away in 1998. Since his departure, Phoenix had plodded through a series of difficult seasons. The 2003–2004 campaign—the season before Steve rejoined the club—was especially dismal. The Suns finished with a record of 29-53, second worst in the Western Conference.

A new Nash, however, meant a new Phoenix Suns. In the 2004–2005 season, Steve led the Suns to an amazing 62 wins. The Suns' 33 additional victories over the previous season marked the third-biggest turnaround in NBA history. The team succeeded mostly on the strength of its high-octane offense: Phoenix averaged 110.4 points per game, more than any team had posted in 10 years. Tom Gugliotta, a 13-year NBA veteran, said of Phoenix's newfound success:

"It's pretty much the same team as last year, but all their big players had career years this year. And there's only one difference: Steve Nash."

Steve with Alejandra Amarilla. He met the Paraguayan-born personal trainer in Manhattan—where they now live during the NBA's off-season—in 2001. Steve and Alejandra were married in 2005 and have twin daughters, Lourdes and Isabella. The Nashes are private people and do not release much information about their personal lives.

Running the offense: Behind Steve's brilliant play at point guard, the Phoenix Suns engineered one of the biggest turnarounds in NBA history in 2004–2005. They finished the regular season with a whopping 62 wins—33 more than the Nash-less Phoenix squad of the previous season had recorded.

Thanks to the skills, confidence, vision, and hard work of the Suns' Canadian superstar, the team went from one of the worst in the league to championship contenders.

⇒ THE 2005 MVP ⇐

Steve's efforts had always led to success for his teams, but at the end of the 2004–2005 season, he was finally recognized for his individual achievements. The Maurice Podoloff Trophy—or the MVP trophy, as it is better known—is the highest honor any basketball player can receive. The winner is selected by a vote of sportswriters and broadcasters throughout the United States and Canada.

At the time, Steve Nash was just the second international player to win MVP honors. Hakeem Olajuwon, a native of Nigeria, was awarded the trophy in 1994. Also, Steve was just the fourth point guard to win the trophy—the others were Bob Cousy, Oscar Robertson, and Magic Johnson. Steve received MVP honors not only because of his remarkable effect on his team's morale and success, but also because of his outstanding individual play. During the regular season, he made over 43 percent of his three-pointers. He also averaged 15.5 points per game and led the league with 11.5 assists per game. After a game in which the Suns had crushed his team, Washington Wizards coach Eddie Jordan commented:

> **"Phoenix is a very good team, a very unselfish team. They pass the ball, and Steve Nash is the ultimate playmaker. Nash is the MVP for reasons we saw tonight."**

Steve was again selected to represent the West in the All-Star Game, and he exhibited his fantastic ball-handling ability by winning the 2005 All-Star Skills Contest, a supplementary competition during the NBA's All-Star Weekend.

⇛ BACK IN PLAYOFF ACTION ⇚

Following their landmark season, the Suns entered the 2005 NBA playoffs as the #1 seed in the Western Conference. They cruised into the second round, where they met Steve's old team, the Dallas Mavericks. Just before Game 1, league officials gave Steve the MVP trophy in front of a cheering Phoenix crowd, his new and old teammates, and Mark Cuban, the Mavericks owner who had let Steve Nash go. Later, Cuban appeared on the *Late Show with David Letterman* and lamented:

> **"And you know Steve's a great guy and I love him to death, but why couldn't he play like an MVP for us?"**

In the first game of the Western Conference Semifinals, Steve proved he deserved the trophy, scoring 11 points, making 13 assists, and leading the Suns to a crushing 127-102 victory. Steve's ability to open up the floor for other players allowed teammate Amare Stoudemire to rack up 40 points. The Suns went on to win the series, four games to two.

The next step was the Western Conference Finals, where the Suns would face the team with the second-best regular-season record in the West, the San Antonio Spurs. Although the Spurs were known as an excellent defensive team, they began the series by beating the Suns at their own high-scoring game. San Antonio won Game 1 by a score of 121-114, then followed up with a 111-108 Game 2 victory and a 102-92 win in Game 3.

Facing elimination, Phoenix came out in Game 4 with renewed energy. The contest stayed close through all four quarters. With just a minute left in the game and Phoenix up by a score of 107-106, Steve Nash, dribbling quickly, weaved toward the basket. Spurs defenders quickly closed in on him and edged him toward the out-of-bounds line. Steve began to fall backwards out of bounds. But just before hitting the floor, he fired a pass to Stoudemire, who made an easy layup. On defense, Stoudemire made an amazing block on a Tim Duncan dunk, and a few seconds later, Steve sealed the 111-106 win by sinking two free throws.

It was a marvelous performance, but the Suns couldn't sustain the momentum. In the next game, the Spurs eliminated Phoenix, 101-95, and went on to claim the NBA crown.

Despite the disappointing end to the season, Suns fans had much reason for optimism. The franchise had made its first trip to the Western Conference Finals since 1993, when the team had been led by Charles Barkley and Kevin Johnson—a golden age the Suns had been trying to return to ever since. And now, with Steve Nash at the helm, it looked as if they were back.

⟫ MVP ELITE ⟪

However, the team suffered a big setback before the start of the 2005–2006 season. In October, during the team's training camp, young star Amare Stoudemire suffered a serious knee injury that caused him to miss almost the entire season.

The Suns rose to the challenge. They powered through the regular season, finishing with a record of 54 wins and 28 losses.

Steve Nash played a huge role in the Suns' success. In addition to keeping the team's offense running smoothly from the point-guard

Josh Howard (left) tries unsuccessfully to block a Steve Nash layup as his Dallas Mavericks teammate Jerry Stackhouse looks on during the fifth game of the Western Conference Semifinals, May 18, 2005. The Suns won the game, 114-108, and went on to win the playoff series, four games to two.

position, Steve put up great individual numbers. For the second year in a row, he was chosen as the NBA's MVP. This put him in elite company: Kareem Abdul-Jabbar, Larry Bird, Wilt Chamberlain, Tim Duncan, Magic Johnson, Michael Jordan, Moses Malone, and Bill Russell are the only other players to win back-to-back MVP awards.

The 2006 Western Conference All-Star team. Seated, from left: Tony Parker, Steve Nash, Ray Allen. Standing, from left: Shawn Marion, Elton Brand, Kevin Garnett, Dirk Nowitzki, Yao Ming, Pau Gasol, Tim Duncan, Tracy McGrady, Kobe Bryant. Behind 29 points from LeBron James, the Eastern Conference team would prevail, 122-120, in the All-Star Game.

⇒ NBA PLAYOFFS 2006 ⇐

Steve continued his second MVP season into the playoffs. In the first round, the Suns faced Kobe Bryant and the Los Angeles Lakers. Opening the series at home, the Suns took Game 1 by a score of 107-102. But Game 2 belonged to the Lakers, 99-93. The series resumed in Los Angeles, with the Lakers having wrested home-court advantage away from the Suns. Los Angeles won Game 3, then followed up with a Game 4 victory on the strength of a Kobe Bryant jump shot at the buzzer.

As the teams headed back to Phoenix to continue the series, the Suns' hopes appeared all but gone. But Phoenix responded with a Game 5 blowout, beating the Lakers 114-97. Game 6 was a tense affair that went into overtime, but Phoenix again staved off elimination behind Steve Nash's 32 points and 13 assists.

The decisive Game 7 was played on May 6. Steve was slowed down a bit after hurting his ankle, but Phoenix jumped out to a 17-point lead in the first quarter and then cruised to a 121-90 victory.

Phoenix met the Los Angeles Clippers in the Western Conference Semifinals. Steve Nash reached deep to overcome his injury, posting 31 points and 12 assists to bring the Suns the win in Game 1. The teams then traded victories and losses until the series was knotted at three games apiece going into Game 7. Steve knew what had to be done: he scored 29 points and tallied 11 assists, and with Shawn Marion and Leandro Barbosa also putting up big numbers, the Suns advanced to the Western Conference Finals.

The Dallas Mavericks, Steve Nash's old team, awaited. In Game 1, Steve again confirmed his MVP status, leading the Suns to victory with 27 points and 16 assists. However, the Mavericks were the more rested team, and it showed. They took the series four games to two. Again Steve's team had made an impressive run but was stopped one step away from the NBA's greatest stage.

Once the almost exclusive domain of Americans, the NBA has truly gone international, drawing talented players from Europe, South America, Africa, Australia, and Asia. NBA basketball is also very popular among sports fans around the world. Evidence of the NBA's global reach can be found on the cover of this Chinese magazine, which features Canadian Steve Nash.

5

His Time Is Now

EVEN INTO HIS THIRTIES, STEVE NASH'S CONTIN-
ued excellence on the court is undeniable—despite
the fact that the ultimate prize, an NBA championship, has eluded him. Between 2004 and 2008, Steve
led the league in total assists and assists per game. His
talents were a large reason his teams led the league in
scoring from 2001 to 2007.

Although he continues to fight persistent back pain, Steve seems
to improve with each passing year. Suns teammate Raja Bell said:

> **He's at a level where there's not much room to
> grow, but when most guys wouldn't be able to
> grow that extra inch, he finds a way to get better
> and mean a little bit more to a team that has more
> weapons than it did last year.**

⇒ MOST VALUABLE PERSONALITY ⇐

After becoming the league's Most Valuable Player, Steve Nash was approached by numerous companies looking for him to endorse their products. Such endorsements could have brought him millions of dollars. However, Steve has very strong views on social responsibility, and he rejected most of the endorsement offers. His sports agent, Bill Duffy, said to the *Sporting News*:

> **"I can think of several big things we have put in front of him, but he is not interested. He has his principles, and we respect that. He has perspective on everything he does."**

Steve has lent his name to companies whose practices are in line with his views on social responsibility and **environmental sustainability**. One such company is Clearly Canadian, which produces flavored sparkling water and funds self-sustaining water sources in Central and South America. Steve also endorses Raymond Weil watches, but all the money he is paid for the endorsement goes to his charitable foundation. Raymond Weil also puts the foundation's logo on its advertisements.

⇒ THE STEVE NASH FOUNDATION ⇐

Instead of using his fame and popularity to enrich himself, Steve has worked very hard to raise money for charities and other **humanitarian** efforts. In 2001, the star point guard began the Steve Nash Foundation, which focuses on children's education and health, adoption, poverty, and environmental awareness (including support for recycling, energy conservation, and environmentally friendly business practices).

The foundation also paid for the establishment of the Hospital de Clínicas in Paraguay, which serves the poor of its community and is Paraguay's only teaching hospital. Although the Steve Nash Foundation mostly serves children and the poor in Arizona, British Columbia, and Paraguay, it is also deeply involved in GuluWalk, a charity that supports and raises money for children displaced and abandoned because of warfare in Uganda.

CROSS-CURRENTS

To learn how Steve and others have used their celebrity for good causes, read "Putting Celebrity in the Service of Charity." Go to page 55. ▶▶

Pass by Steve.
Body by milk.

Off the court, milk provides the perfect assist.
Its protein helps build muscle and studies suggest teens who choose
milk over sugary drinks tend to be leaner. Staying active,
eating right and drinking three glasses of lowfat or fat free milk a day
helps you look great and stay in shape. Score three for milk.

got milk?

STEVE NASH ©2007 AMERICA'S MILK PROCESSORS

bodybymilk.com

Steve Nash jumped on a trampoline to get this shot for the "Got Milk?" ad campaign encouraging kids to drink milk. "When you look at all the people who have played a part in this campaign over the years," Steve said, "it's a thrill and an honor to be one of them."

STEVE NASH

Steve believes in supporting peace, health, and general awareness of the issues affecting the people of the world. Commenting on his philosophy, he said:

> **"I am a huge believer in giving back and helping out in the community and the world. Think globally, act locally I suppose. I believe that the measure of a person's life is the effect they have on others. "**

Steve Nash autographs T-shirts for kids before the Steve Nash Foundation Charity Classic, held at the Air Canada Centre in Vancouver, British Columbia, July 21, 2007. Steve first organized the annual event—which brings together NBA stars for a basketball game—in 2005. Proceeds from the game benefit underprivileged children.

Steve uses what he knows best—basketball—to help raise awareness of the issues important to him. Since 2005, he has organized the Steve Nash Foundation Charity Classic, which is supported by local and international sponsors and gathers NBA stars together for a game of basketball and a day of games for children.

In 2007, Steve was involved in a similar event, but this time it was held on the other side of the world. He and Houston Rockets star Yao Ming organized a charity basketball match in Beijing, China. Other NBA stars, including Carmelo Anthony, Baron Davis, and Yi Jianlian, joined them to play in the game. Through the game, along with a banquet afterward, Steve and Yao were able to raise over $2.5 million for poor children in China.

ENDORSING HEALTH

Growing up in an athletic family and having an athletic family of his own (his wife is a personal trainer), Steve understands the need for children to be active and healthy. In 2001, he began the Steve Nash Youth Basketball League in British Columbia; it has since attracted about 10,000 young players.

Steve also recognizes that adults need exercise to stay healthy. He began the Steve Nash Sports Club in Vancouver, British Columbia. In keeping with Steve's dedication to sustainability, its design incorporates more efficient lighting.

Recently, Steve has promised to support the new Professional Women's Soccer League, which is scheduled to begin play in the spring of 2009. His soccer roots and his two young daughters likely influenced his decision to help finance the league, and he told *Canadian Press*:

> **"I'm looking forward to it getting off the ground. I want to be a big fan and hopefully watch them not only entertain but inspire lots of young girls and kids in general."**

THE ALMOST THREE-PEAT

After two straight appearances in the Western Conference Finals and two straight losses there, the Suns again mixed up their roster by trading players. The team and its fans were also very happy to have Amare Stoudemire healthy again.

AND OPENING JULY 2007 VANCOUVER BC

On July 19, 2007, ribbon-cutting ceremonies were held to officially open the Steve Nash Sports Club in Vancouver. The club reflects Steve's belief that exercise is essential to a healthy lifestyle. In keeping with his commitment to the environment, the facilities incorporate design features such as energy-efficient lighting.

In the 2006–2007 regular season, Steve led the Suns to a record of 61 wins and 21 losses, the third-best record in the franchise's history. He also became the first player since Magic Johnson in 1991 to average at least 18 points and 11 assists in a season.

When the voting for the league MVP came to a close, Nash was only a tiny bit behind the eventual winner and one of his best friends—Dirk Nowitzki. Nowitzki, who was just the third international player named league MVP, had led his Dallas Mavericks squad to a record of 67 wins and 15 losses, which ranked in the top 10 best records in NBA history.

⟫ CANADA'S STAR ⟪

In October of 2007, Steve received a very special honor from his native Canada. He was appointed an Officer of the Order of Canada, which is the country's highest civilian honor. The award "recognizes a lifetime of outstanding achievement, dedication to the community and service to the nation." Steve received the award because of his charitable activities, his demonstrations of goodwill, and his success in the NBA—and because he conducts himself responsibly in his professional and private life.

Steve Nash is unquestionably Canada's greatest basketball star ever. But in his native land he is just as well known for his off-court charitable work as for his on-court heroics. The Canadian government recognized Steve's "lifetime of outstanding achievement, dedication to the community, and service to the nation" by awarding him the country's highest civilian honor in October 2007.

But this was not the first Canadian award Steve had received. In May of 2006, he was inducted into the Order of British Columbia, which in the highest civilian honor for Steve's home province. Other winners include the world-famous jazz singer Diana Krall, hockey star Trevor Linden, and singer-songwriter Sarah McLachlan.

In 2005 and 2006, Steve also won the Lionel Conacher Award, which is the trophy given to the best male athlete in Canada. Hockey stars such as Wayne Gretzky, Bobby Hull, Mario Lemieux, and Bobby Orr have also won the award, as have sprinter Ben Johnson and auto racer Jacques Villeneuve. In 2005, a committee of Canadian sportswriters selected Steve for another honor: the Lou Marsh Trophy, given to the Canadian athlete of the year.

➤ HUNTING THE GREATEST PRIZE ◀

Steve's trophy case may be filled with awards and honors—both for his heroics on the basketball court and his humanitarian work off it. But he desperately wants one more prize: an NBA championship. When asked if he would rather have a third MVP trophy or a championship ring, Steve said:

> **"Oh, are you kidding? I'd trade all three for a championship."**

Early in 2008, the Suns made what was arguably their biggest move since getting Steve Nash—they traded with the Miami Heat for Shaquille O'Neal. A 16-year veteran, Shaq has abundant championship experience (he won three titles with the Lakers and one with the Heat). Although Shaq can dominate in the paint—both defensively and offensively—some Phoenix fans were concerned that he wouldn't be a good fit with the team's offensive scheme. Specifically, they thought that the big man would slow down Phoenix's run-and-gun, transition offense. This, they worried, would add up to fewer rather than more victories.

During the stretch drive, these concerns appeared unwarranted. Phoenix won 10 of the remaining 15 regular-season games after Shaq made his debut with the club on February 10. It finished the season with a solid record of 55-27. But for Phoenix, the playoffs proved a major disappointment. The defending NBA champion San Antonio Spurs dispatched the Suns, four games to one, in the first round.

Steve Nash (left) runs the Phoenix Suns' half-court offense in a game against the Denver Nuggets, March 31, 2008. Phoenix won the contest, 132-117, to notch its 50th victory of the season. Although the Suns went on to win 55 games, Steve's dreams of a championship were again thwarted, as his team was bounced in the first round of the playoffs.

Steve Nash has come a long way from his childhood in Victoria, British Columbia. Through hard work and determination, Steve has made the most of his athletic gifts, becoming one of the NBA's best point guards. In using his fame to advance a variety of worthy causes, Steve has become something else as well: a role model.

Like Shaquille O'Neal, Steve Nash is probably in the final few years of his professional basketball career. Some NBA observers believe the chances that he will win a championship ring are becoming more and more remote. Eleven-time NBA champion Bill Russell disagrees. Russell observed:

> **"I will say this—first of all, his career is not over. A lot of guys that won championships, they won it after their prime."**

Steve Nash's contract with the Phoenix Suns runs out at end of the 2011–2012 season, when he will be 37 years old. He might not be in peak physical condition then, but he will still be one of the smartest players in the game. Steve will still have a lot to offer any team, as a point guard who gets limited playing time or as a role model and mentor for young players.

Time inevitably erodes the skills of every athlete. But Steve Nash appears to be aging gracefully. In 2008, he was named an NBA All-Star for the sixth time. He finished the 2007–2008 season with stellar stats. Steve averaged nearly 17 points per game. He connected on more than 50 percent of his total field goal attempts, including a career-best 47 percent of his three-point attempts. Only Jason Kapono of the Toronto Raptors was more accurate from three-point range. Steve's 11.1 assists per game was also second in the NBA (Chris Paul of the New Orleans Hornets averaged 11.6 dishes per game).

Steve Nash's versatility and his willingness to adapt his game to suit the needs of his team help make him one of the best point guards in the NBA. These qualities also suggest that, as long as the man from Canada puts on a uniform and takes to the court, he will always be in the hunt for the NBA's greatest prize.

MVPs in Multiples

As of 2008, only 11 men had been named the NBA's Most Valuable Player more than once. Big men dominate this list. Aside from Steve Nash, only two other guards have garnered multiple MVP awards: Magic Johnson and Michael Jordan.

At 6 feet 9 inches, three-time MVP Magic Johnson was very tall for a point guard. In his 13-year career with the Los Angeles Lakers, Johnson was a 12-time All-Star and helped lead the Lakers to five NBA championships.

Michael Jordan, a 6'6" shooting guard with incredible leaping ability, was named league MVP five times. Jordan played 15 seasons, all but two of them with the Chicago Bulls, a team he helped lead to six championships. He was the NBA's leading scorer 10 times, led in steals three times, and played in 14 All-Star games. Some basketball authorities consider Jordan the best player of all time.

Others believe that distinction belongs to Wilt Chamberlain, a 7'1" center awarded four MVP trophies, including three straight during the 1960s. Chamberlain, who won championships with the Philadelphia 76ers and the Los Angeles Lakers, posted some incredible offensive statistics during his 14 seasons in the NBA. He once scored 100 points in a game—which remains an NBA record. His career points-per-game average (30.07) remains second only to that of Jordan (30.12),

and his 22.89 rebounds per game is best all time.

Chamberlain had many legendary duels with 6'10" Boston Celtics center Bill Russell, a five-time MVP. Russell didn't equal Chamberlain in offensive output, but he was a great rebounder, shot blocker, and passer. And during his career, which extended from 1956 to 1969, Russell helped lead the Celtics to an incredible 11 NBA championships.

Kareem Abdul-Jabbar also anchored a dynasty—the Los Angeles Lakers of the 1980s, which won five NBA championships. In addition, he won a title with the Milwaukee Bucks in 1971. Abdul-Jabbar, a 7'2" center, is the only six-time MVP in NBA history. Over the course of his 20-year career, he scored 38,387 regular-season points, more than any other player.

Other players who won multiple MVP trophies are Boston Celtics forward Larry Bird, an outstanding all-around player who won the award three consecutive years (1984, 1985, 1986); center Moses Malone, who won one MVP with the Houston Rockets (1979) and two with the Philadelphia 76ers (1982, 1983); San Antonio Spurs forward/center Tim Duncan (MVP in 2002 and 2003); Utah Jazz forward Karl Malone (1997, 1999); and St. Louis Hawks forward/center Bob Pettit (1956, 1959).

(Go back to page 9.)

Michael Jordan rises up for a trademark slam dunk in a game against the Orlando Magic. In his 15-year NBA career, Jordan—arguably the best basketball player in history—won five MVP awards. One other player—Boston Celtics center Bill Russell—matched that mark, and only Milwaukee Bucks/Los Angeles Lakers center Kareem Abdul-Jabbar exceeded it, with six MVPs in his career.

March Madness

In Steve Nash's freshman year, the Santa Clara Broncos finished third in the West Coast Conference and earned a spot in the 1993 National Collegiate Athletic Association (NCAA) men's basketball championships. The Broncos were a #15 seed. A "seed" is basically a ranking that determines where a team appears in a tournament bracket and who the team will play. Most tournaments are organized so that the lowest seed plays the highest seed in the first round. The idea is to have the best teams, if they are not upset by a lower seed, play against each other toward the end of the tournament.

The year 1993 marked Santa Clara's first appearance in the NCAA tournament since 1970. And Steve Nash and the Broncos did their part to see that the tournament earned its popular nickname of "March Madness": they pulled off a huge first-round upset, beating the University of Arizona, a #2 seed, by a score of 64-61. It was only the second time in tournament history that a #15 seed had defeated a #2 seed. Steve showed steely nerves and a confidence

Each year, fans of college basketball eagerly await the arrival of March. That's when the NCAA basketball tournament—March Madness—kicks off. With 64 of the best teams in the country competing for the collegiate championship in a single-elimination format, the excitement is intense, and upsets are a virtual certainty.

unexpected in a freshman by sinking six of six free throws in the last 30 seconds of the game.

(Go back to page 14.)

In with the New

The players eligible for a specific NBA draft are known as a "draft class." The term relates to graduating classes in school, because the idea is that basketball players are, when they enter the draft, graduating to a new level of competition, experience, and skill. Many draft classes feature a lot of promising players. But rarely has a class delivered so many players who have gone on to NBA superstardom as the class of 1996. In addition to Steve Nash, the 1996 draft class produced, among others, Allen Iverson, Marcus Camby, Stephon Marbury, Ray Allen, Kobe Bryant, and Jermaine O'Neal.

While acknowledging the accomplishments of the star-studded class of 1996, some basketball experts believe that the 2003 draft class was the most talented in NBA history. Among the players drafted that year were LeBron James, Darko Milicic, Carmelo Anthony, Chris Bosh, Dwyane Wade, Chris Kaman, Kirk Hinrich, and T. J. Ford. These players have already made a mark on the NBA. But the argument as to which class, 2003 or 1996, was better will probably not be settled for years, when the players have retired and are eligible for induction into the Basketball Hall of Fame. (Go back to page 14.) ◀◀

Los Angeles Lakers guard Kobe Bryant jams the ball home. Bryant, drafted into the NBA right out of high school, was the 13th pick in the 1996 draft. Some basketball experts consider that draft the best ever: in addition to Bryant, it included Allen Iverson, Steve Nash, Jermaine O'Neal, Ray Allen, Peja Stojakovic, and Stephon Marbury.

Statistics of Dominance

In basketball, as in most other professional sports, players are frequently judged by their individual statistics. Obviously, stats cannot tell the whole story, but the numbers do help identify outstanding performers.

In the NBA, the double-double—when a player records 10 or more in any two of the five basic categories (points, assists, rebounds, blocks, and steals)—is regarded as a good statistical indicator of a solid game. Karl Malone holds the all-time career record for double-doubles, with 782. In the 2006–2007 season, Steve Nash was one of just six players to average a double-double over the entire season.

Earning a triple-double (recording 10 or more in three of the above categories) is much rarer. It shows a player's dominance in a single game. Oscar Robertson holds the all-time record for triple-doubles, with 181. The next highest is Magic Johnson, with 138. Robertson is also the only player in NBA history to average a triple-double for a whole season, which he did in 1961–1962.

If a triple-double is a rare occurrence, a quadruple-double (10 or more in four of the five categories) is nearly unheard of. Only four players have ever recorded a quadruple-double: Hakeem Olajuwon, Alvin Robertson, David Robinson, and Nate Thurmond. (Go back to page 19.) ◀◀

Oscar Robertson of the Milwaukee Bucks dribbles the ball in a game against the Los Angeles Lakers, early 1970s. In 1996, the NBA named the 50 Greatest Players in NBA History. Robertson's name was on the list. The Hall of Fame guard finished his career averaging 25.7 points per game. One season he averaged a triple-double.

World Hoops

The "Dream Team" of NBA stars that represented the United States at the 1992 Summer Olympics in Barcelona, Spain, did much to increase the popularity of basketball worldwide. The team beat its opponents by an average of 44 points per game en route to the gold medal. Seen here at the medal ceremony are (from left) Scottie Pippen, Michael Jordan, and Clyde Drexler.

The Summer Olympics first included men's basketball in 1936 (women's basketball was added in 1976). Since then the competition has been for the most part dominated by the United States. NBA players have been allowed to compete in the Olympics only since 1992. In the 1992 Summer Olympics in Barcelona, Spain, the United States formed the "Dream Team," one of the best teams the world has ever seen. On average the Dream Team—which included Charles Barkley, Larry Bird, Clyde Drexler, Patrick Ewing, Magic Johnson, Michael Jordan, Christian Laettner, Karl Malone, Chris Mullin, Scottie Pippen, David Robinson, and John Stockton—outscored its Olympic opponents by 44 points.

Canada sent a team to Berlin, Germany, in 1936 to participate in basketball's Olympic debut, and the Canadians won the silver medal, finishing second only to the United States. Since then, however, Canada has failed to win another medal. Its best performances were fourth-place finishes in 1976 and 1984.

In addition to representing Canada at the 2000 Summer Olympics in Sydney, Steve Nash played with the Canadian national team in 2004. But the team failed to qualify for the Olympic Games held in Athens, Greece, that year. A short time after Canadian officials announced a coaching change, Steve commented that he would probably not again play for Canada in the Olympics. (Go back to page 20.) ◀◀

Running Point

The role of a point guard is to make plays. The best point guards have multiple weapons. They are excellent ball handlers and passers. They can score from the outside or penetrate to the basket. Most important, they can take control of an offense and make their entire team better.

Steve Nash is one of the premier point guards of his era. His skills, court awareness, and leadership bring to mind some of the game's all-time greats at the point-guard position.

Nate Archibald, nicknamed "Tiny," was famous for his creativity, intelligence, and speed. During the 1972–1973 season, he became the only player in NBA history to lead the league in both scoring and assists. Tiny won one NBA championship. Off the court, he devoted much of his time to improving the lives of children and poor people in his native New York City.

Bob Cousy, league MVP in 1957, was a master at running the offense. His no-look passes and slick dribbling confused defenders and set the bar for future point guards. Playing on the dominant Celtics teams of the 1950s and early 1960s, Cousy won six NBA titles.

Walt Frazier, famous for his quickness and smooth style of play, was a believer in strong defense and passing. He spent 10 of his 13 NBA seasons with the New York Knicks, helping the team win two titles.

John Stockton is regarded by some people as the best passer in NBA history. He holds the NBA records for the most career assists, the most assists in a single season, and the highest average assists in a single season, with 14.5 per game. Stockton also led the league in assists for nine consecutive seasons. He was part of the Dream Team in 1992, but he never won an MVP trophy or an NBA championship.

Among current players, Jason Kidd ranks with Steve Nash as one of the most respected point guards. His strong defense and accurate passes make him a valuable contributor and leader. Kidd's NBA career began in 1994, and that season he shared Rookie of the Year honors with Grant Hill. Since then, Kidd has been named an All-Star nine times. He ranks fifth all-time in assists per game and total assists, and he is number one in both of those categories among active players.

(Go back to page 28.)

Putting Celebrity in the Service of Charity

Professional basketball enjoys immense popularity around the world, and the NBA is the premier league. Many NBA players have found that stardom on the court translates into status as an international celebrity.

This high profile has some drawbacks. For example, players generally have less privacy, as many avid fans and the **paparazzi** are obsessed with keeping track of what the players do off the court.

But fame also brings opportunities to make even more money through product endorsements. Some players have certainly cashed in those opportunities.

Other players have used their fame not for personal gain but to advance social goals they believe in. After winning his first MVP award, Steve Nash recognized that his celebrity status gave his charities immediate and immense visibility, and he was able to recruit other celebrities to his causes. For the UNICEF "Unite for Children, Unite Against AIDS" campaign in 2006, Steve was joined by NBA players Elton Brand, Pau Gasol, LeBron James, Andrei Kirilenko, Yao Ming, Dikembe Mutombo, and Dirk Nowitzki, and by WNBA players Swin Cash

In 2007, Steve Nash approached Houston Rockets center Yao Ming with the idea of playing a pair of exhibition games to benefit charity in Yao's native China. Steve led a team of NBA stars against a team of Chinese stars captained by Yao. The games helped raise $2.5 million to build schools in impoverished rural China.

and Becky Hammon. These athletes were also joined by newscaster Katie Couric and actors Orlando Bloom, Laurence Fishburne, Sarah Jessica Parker, and Edward James Olmos.

(Go back to page 38.)

1974   Stephen John Nash is born in Johannesburg, South Africa, on February 7.

1992   Leads St. Michael's University School in Victoria to the British Columbia AAA
               Provincial Championship in basketball.

1996   Is drafted 15th overall by the Phoenix Suns and enters the NBA.

1998   Traded to the Dallas Mavericks.

1999   Suffers a terrible back sprain that causes chronic pain.

2000   Plays in his first Olympics and leads the Canadian basketball team to its
               best record in 50 years.

2001   Appears in his first NBA playoffs.

2002   Appears in his first NBA All-Star Game.

2004   Becomes a free agent and accepts an offer from the Phoenix Suns.

               On October 14, becomes a father to twin girls.

2005   Is named Most Valuable Player of the NBA.

               In June, marries Alejandra Amarilla, his longtime girlfriend and the mother
               of his daughters.

2006   Wins second consecutive MVP award.

2007   Narrowly misses winning his third consecutive MVP trophy.

               With Yao Ming, organizes a very successful charity event in Beijing for
               poor Chinese children.

2008   Receives his sixth All-Star selection.

Personal Awards

British Columbia Basketball Player of the Year (1992)

British Columbia Soccer Player of the Year (1992)

West Coast Conference Player of the Year (1995, 1996)

NBA All-Star (2002, 2003, 2005, 2006, 2007, 2008)

All-NBA 3rd Team (2002, 2003)

All-NBA 1st Team (2005, 2006, 2007)

NBA MVP (2005, 2006)

Lou Marsh Trophy (2005)

Lionel Conacher Award (2005, 2006)

Order of British Columbia (2006)

Order of Canada (2007)

Career Statistics

Year	Team	Minutes per Game	Field Goal %	3-Point %	Free Throw %	Assists per Game	Points per Game
1996–97	PHO	10.5	.423	.418	.824	2.1	3.3
1997–98	PHO	21.9	.459	.415	.860	3.4	9.1
1998–99	DAL	31.7	.363	.374	.826	5.5	7.9
1999–00	DAL	27.4	.477	.403	.882	4.9	8.6
2000–01	DAL	34.1	.487	.406	.895	7.3	15.6
2001–02	DAL	34.6	.483	.455	.887	7.7	17.9
2002–03	DAL	33.1	.465	.413	.909	7.3	17.7
2003–04	DAL	33.5	.470	.405	.916	8.8	14.5
2004–05	PHO	34.3	.502	.431	.887	11.5	15.5
2005–06	PHO	35.5	.512	.439	.921	10.5	18.8
2006–07	PHO	35.3	.532	.455	.899	11.6	18.6
2007–08	PHO	34.3	.504	.470	.906	11.1	16.9
Totals:		30.8	.485	.431	.897	7.9	14.3

Books

Arseneault, Paul. *Steve Nash*. British Columbia, Canada: Heritage House Publishing, 2006.

Bailey, Peter. *Steve Nash: Most Valuable Player*. Bolton, Ontario, Canada: Fenn Publishing, 2007.

Basen, Ryan. *Steve Nash: Leader On and Off the Court*. Berkeley Heights, NJ: Enslow Publishers, 2007.

Hareas, John. *Steve Nash*. New York: Scholastic, 2008.

Rud, Jeff. *Steve Nash: The Making of an MVP, with a Foreword by Steve Nash*. New York: Puffin, 2007.

Savage, Jeff. *Steve Nash*. Minneapolis: Lerner Publications, 2006.

Web Sites

http://www.nba.com/playerfile/steve_nash/bio.html
The NBA's site for statistics and write-ups about Steve Nash.

http://www.basketball-reference.com/players/n/nashst01.html
In-depth statistics on Steve Nash.

http://www.nba.com/history/players/index.html
Short biographies and statistics for some of the best players in NBA history.

http://stevenash.org/html/main.html
The home page of the Steve Nash Foundation.

http://www.nba.com/games/20050509/DALPHO/recap.html
Offers a summary of specific playoff games.

apartheid—a former policy of segregation and political and economic discrimination against non-European groups in the Republic of South Africa.

double-double—an instance in which a basketball player records 10 or more in two of five categories (points, assists, rebounds, blocks, or steals) in a single game.

environmental sustainability—the use of natural resources in a way that does not harm the environment or deplete or permanently damage the resources.

field goal—a basket, worth two or three points (depending on where on the court the player shoots the ball).

franchise—a team and its organization within a league.

free throw—an undefended shot from behind a set line, which is awarded as the result of a foul and is worth one point.

humanitarian—a person who promotes human welfare and social reform.

netball—a sport similar to basketball but with a basket mounted on the top of a pole and without a backboard; the court is also divided into zones that are restricted to certain player positions.

paparazzi—photographers who aggressively pursue celebrities for the purpose of taking candid photos.

point guard—a basketball player assigned to run his team's offense.

seed—a team that has been ranked for the purpose of competing in a tournament.

set offense—any basketball offense that involves the use of a series of predetermined plays, which begin with each of the five players at a specific area of the floor.

transition offense—an offense designed to push the ball quickly up court (after an opponent's missed shot) and to get an easy shot before the defense can set itself.

triple-double—an instance in which a basketball player records 10 or more in three of five categories (points, assists, rebounds, blocks, or steals) in a single game.

underdog—a predicted loser in a contest or struggle.

vertebra—one of the bony segments of the spinal column that encloses the spinal cord.

Chapter 1: Kid Canadian Becomes Mr. MVP

page 6 "[Steve is] one of . . ." "Steve Nash," *Scholastic Action* 31, no. 8 (2008), p. 4.

page 9 "A lot is made about . . ." "Hoser Makes Hoops History, Again," CBC Sports Online, May 8, 2006. http://www.cbc.ca/sports/columns/newsmakers/steve_nash.html.

page 9 "I just try to . . . " Interview, *The Charlie Rose Show*, PBS, August 27, 2007.

Chapter 2: The Rising Star

page 12 "Playing [soccer], I was always . . ." Ian Whittell, "Nash Thinks on His Feet to Earn Spurs with Internet Generation," Times Online, November 19, 2007. http://www.timesonline.co.uk/tol/sport/us_sport/article2895771.ece

page 12 "A coach told me . . ." Sean Gregory, "A Dash of Nash," *Time* (Canadian edition) 165, no. 20 (2005), p. 46.

page 14 "We'd practice all day . . ." Sean Deveney, "Headstrong," *Sporting News* 226, no. 6 (2002), p. 44.

page 14 "He used to drill . . ." Gregory, "Dash of Nash," p. 46.

Chapter 3: From Dallas to the World

page 17 "I didn't take it . . ." Gregory, "Dash of Nash," p. 46.

page 20 "I really don't care . . ." Deveney, "Headstrong," p. 44.

page 25 "I think a lot . . ." John Hollinger, "Steve Speaks Out: Mavericks' Star Voices Opposition to War in Iraq," *SI.com*, February 7, 2003. http://sportsillustrated.cnn.com/basketball/nba/2003/all_star/news/2003/02/07/nash_war/

page 25 "[Phoenix] wanted me . . ." Gregory, "Dash of Nash," p. 46.

Chapter 4: The Valley of the Sun

page 28 "When you think . . ." Sean Deveney, "Pace Pushers," *Sporting News* 228, no. 49 (2004), p. 24.

page 28 "It's pretty much . . ." Gregory, "Dash of Nash," p. 46.

page 31 "Phoenix is a very good . . ." Liz Robbins, "NBA: Suns Guard Would Trade All His Trophies for a Ring," *International Herald Tribune*, January 25, 2007. http://www.iht.com/articles/2007/01/25/sports/nash.php?page=1

page 31 "And you know Steve's . . ." Chuck Carlton, "Cuban Takes His Act to Letterman," *Dallas Morning News*, June 15, 2006. http://www.dallasnews.com/sharedcontent/dws/spt/basketball/mavs/stories/061506dnspoletterman.e9ce.html

Chapter 5: His Time Is Now

page 37 "He's at a level . . ." Robbins, "NBA: Suns Guard Would Trade."

page 38 "I can think of several . . ." Deveney, "Headstrong," p. 44.

page 40 "I am a huge believer . . ." http://www.brainyquote.com/quotes/quotes/s/stevenash191496.html

page 41 "I'm looking forward . . ." Associated Press, "Suns' Nash Invests in New Women's Soccer League," *ESPNsoccernet*, February 4, 2008. http://soccernet.espn.go.com /news/story?id=505170&cc=5901

page 44 "Oh, are you kidding . . ." Robbins, "NBA: Suns Guard Would Trade."

page 47 "I will say this . . ." Ibid.

Ian Kimmich is the author of a novel and numerous short stories. He is also a book editor and lives in Portland, Oregon.

PICTURE CREDITS

page

1: SCU/CIC Photos

4: NBAE/Getty Images

7: Fort Worth Star-Telegram/MCT

8: NBAE/Getty Images

10: Adam Spangler/CIC Photos

13: Craig Hacker/TSN/Icon SMI

15: NBAE/Getty Images

16: SportsChrome Pix

19: Dallas Morning News/KRT

21: UPI Photos

22: Dallas Morning News/KRT

24: Sports Xtra/NMI

26: NBAE/Getty Images

29: NBA/PRMS

30: UPI Photos

33: NBAE/Getty Images

34: NBAE/Getty Images

36: NBA Stuff/NMI

39: Milk PEP/NMI

40: NBAE/Getty Images

42: UrbanMixer/CIC Photos

43: Phoenix Suns/PRMS

45: Ellessu/CIC Photos

46: NBA/PRMS

49: SportsChrome Pix

50: Sports Illustrated/NMI

51: Tim Sloan/AFP Photos

52: SportsChrome Pix

53: Getty Images

55: ColorChinaPhoto

Front cover: NBAE/Getty Images